Books in This Series

Better Baseball for Boys

Better Basketball for Boys

Better Basketball for Girls

Better Bicycling for Boys and Girls

Better BMX Riding and Racing for Boys and Girls

Better Boxing for Boys

Better Cross-Country Running for Boys and Girls

Better Field Events for Girls

Better Field Hockey for Girls

Better Football for Boys

Better Gymnastics for Girls

Better Horseback Riding for Boys and Girls

Better Ice Skating for Boys and Girls

Better Karate for Boys

Better Roller Skating for Boys and Girls

Better Skateboarding for Boys and Girls

Better Soccer for Boys and Girls

Better Softball for Boys and Girls

Better Swimming for Boys and Girls

Better Synchronized Swimming for Girls

Better Tennis for Boys and Girls

Better Track for Girls

Better Volleyball for Girls

Better Weight Training for Boys

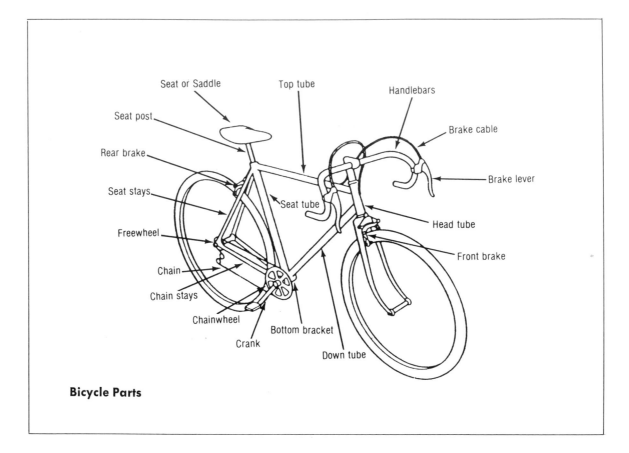

Seat or Saddle

Top tube

Handlebars

Seat post

Brake cable

Rear brake

Brake lever

Seat stays

Seat tube

Freewheel

Head tube

Chain

Front brake

Chain stays

Chainwheel

Bottom bracket

Crank

Down tube

Bicycle Parts

BETTER BICYCLING

for Boys and Girls

George Sullivan

New and Completely Updated Edition

DODD, MEAD & COMPANY · NEW YORK

Many people contributed in the pr̶ ̶ ̶ ̶ ̶DITS
this book. Special thanks are due: P̶ ̶ ̶ ̶ ̶w York Council, American Youth Hostels, 6,
Metropolitan New York Council, Am̶ ̶ ̶ ̶ New York Public Library, 7, 14; Skidlid, 38
Hostels; Jim Hayes, Executive Dir̶e̶ ̶ ̶ ̶ws, 11. All other photographs are by George
Manufacturers of America; James Pere̶ ̶ ̶ ̶piece diagram, Herb Field Art Studio.
Ballard, Midtown Bicycles, New York City; John
Kirkpatrick, Ross Bicycles; Lou Maltese, Century
Road Club Association; Susan Weaver, *Bicycling*;
Sandy Benson, Raleigh Cycle Company of America;
Herb Field, Herb Field Art Studio; and Francesca
Kurti, TLC Custom Labs.

The author is also grateful to the many individuals who posed for the photos that appear in the book, especially Suzanne Musho, and also Bruno Botti, Earl (Goose) Powell, and Ted Wallace.

Distributed in Canada by
McClelland and Stewart Limited, Toronto
Manufactured in the United States of America

1   2   3   4   5   6   7   8   9   10

Library of Congress Cataloging in Publication Data

Sullivan, George, date
  Better bicycling for boys and girls.

  Summary: A guide to successful cycling, including tips on choosing the right bike, buying accessory equipment, cycling safety, bike maintenance, and touring and racing.
  1. Cycling—Juvenile literature. 2. Bicycles—Juvenile literature. [1. Bicycles and bicycling] I. Title.
GV1043.5.S9 1984   629.2'272   84-13650
ISBN 0-396-08476-1
ISBN 0-396-08479-6

CONTENTS

Annual 36-mile bike tour of New York City attracts upwards of 15,000 cyclists.

RIDING, TOURING, RACING

Bicycling is one of the most popular sports in the nation, right up there with swimming and jogging, and way ahead of such standbys as basketball and baseball. About 100 million Americans ride bikes.

Bicycling's popularity is not hard to understand. Bikes are easy to operate; indeed, young children can ride as skillfully as adults.

Bike's don't pollute. And used regularly and with enough vigor, the bike can have important fitness values.

Bicycling got its start in America slightly more than a century ago. During the early 1870s, some of the wealthiest Americans of the time began importing bicycles from England. Recognizing there was money to be made, Colonel Albert Pope established the Pope Manufacturing Company and began producing the first American bicycles. Pope sold his bicycles under the "Columbia" brand name, which is still seen today.

By the early 1900s, more than four million Americans owned two-wheelers, quite an impressive statistic when one considers that all roads at the time were dirt roads and the nation's population was less than one-third of what it is today.

One difference between bicycles then and now is the many uses to which they are being put. The bike has always been used for transportation, of course, for going to and from the store, school, or work. The bicycle has always been important for

Club cyclists of the 1890s

recreation, too, for neighborhood spins with one's friends.

But today, bicycles are frequently used for touring or camping. There is also increasing interest in competitive cycling, in both road racing and track racing. And don't overlook BMX riding and racing, an entirely new branch of the sport.

BIKE TOURING—Touring is taking any journey on a bicycle. How long a journey? You can tour for an afternoon by yourself, traveling perhaps ten or fifteen miles. At the other end of the scale is the planned summer-long tour covering thousands of miles in this country or abroad. One organization, American Youth Hostels (see below) sponsors more than 150 different exciting bicycling, backpacking, canoeing, and sailing trips each summer, ranging from one to ten weeks through the United States, Canada, Europe, or Asia.

Whether the tour is a long or short one, traveling in a group has many advantages. You can ride with whom you please during the day, and then join the groups in the evening to share supper and experiences. In the case of trouble or breakdown on the road, there are plenty of people to help.

The moderate speed at which touring groups travel allows members to drink in all that surrounds them. "When you're riding in a car or on a train, all you experience is the car or the train," says one young rider. "But on a bike you really experience all that is going on around you—the trees, the flowers, the sky, the air. You're part of things."

Many groups and organizations will help you plan your bike tour. One of the foremost is American Youth Hostels, or AYH, for short. (Consult Chapter 10 for the address of American Youth Hostels, as well as for the addresses of other organizations mentioned in this book.) AYH is a nonprofit organization with the aim of encouraging people "to enjoy the out-of-doors . . .and to travel simply and inexpensively, staying at hostels." What is a hostel? It's simply an overnight accommodation in a setting that is likely to be scenic, cultural, or historical. A hostel can be a school not in use, a church, old barn, former Navy barracks, a lighthouse, modern building, or even some specially built facility.

The AYH offers some 5,000 hostels in 51 countries. There are over 300 in the United States, and about 100,000 people—AYH members—are authorized to use them. Fees for an overnight stay

Touring cyclists on Cape Cod; house in background is their hostel.

are never more than a few dollars.

Hosteling is popular in Canada, too. For more information, write the Canadian Hosteling Association.

Most clubs and organizations such as AYH consider a local trip to be one that covers about 20 miles. It usually has a destination that has historical, geographical, or cultural interest. It can take in local parks, zoos, or sites of historical or architectural interest, or college or university campuses.

Novice tours are those that cover 40 to 60 miles in a period of two days, usually over a weekend. You may camp out, stay at a hostel, or rent a room overnight. Intermediate tours are those that last up to a week and include several different overnight stops.

Advanced trips are longer than a week in duration. They're not for the beginner rider, however, because they require more than the usual amount of stamina.

8

The amount of equipment you'll require depends on the kind of trip you're taking and its length. A good guideline to follow suggests that you carry as little as possible but as much as necessary.

Two saddlebags, called "panniers," slung over a rear rack, should be enough to carry the bulk of your supplies. Try to distribute the weight evenly in the panniers and keep the center of gravity as low as possible for better balance.

A handlebar sack is also useful. Be sure it attaches securely. A bag that jiggles can be very annoying.

Before you actually take part in a tour, be sure you are in first-class physical condition. Once you're on the road, plan to eat moderately, stressing foods that are high in nutritional value, such as nuts, grains, dried fruit, and the like.

A bicycle that is being used to tote camping gear has to be ridden in a different manner than an unloaded bike. You have to be able to brake faster and, when approaching an uphill grade, shift sooner. You can't bank quite as sharply when rounding corners.

Most important, you must never attempt to exceed what you're capable of doing in terms of physical ability. Do so and you may let yourself in for an experience that seems as if it's from a Stephen King movie. Otherwise, the trip can be a fun-filled adventure, an enriching experience that you will remember for the rest of your life.

BICYCLE RACING—Competitors in bicycle racing attain the highest speed achieved by man while

Cyclists carry all that is necessary.

traveling under his own power. The all-time record was established in 1962 by Antonio Maspes of Italy who covered a 200-meter course (about 219

9

yards) in 10.6 seconds, a speed of 42.2 miles per hour.

What's good about bicycle racing is that you compete according to your age, sex, and the amount of cycling experience you have. That means you don't have to worry about being beaten badly the first time out.

Also don't worry about your size—or lack of it. Some of the best riders are small in stature. The less weight you have to lug, the better.

There are both road races and track races, and several different kinds of each.

One form of road racing is the time trial. In this, the winner is the rider who covers a measured course—10, 25, 50, or 100 miles—in the fastest time. Riders start at one-minute intervals. The record for the 25-mile race is approximately 50 minutes, an average speed of around 27 miles an hour.

The massed start is another type of race. It is similar to a cross-country footrace, with everyone starting together. The winner is the first rider to cross the finish line. Single-day massed-start races are between 50 and 100 miles in length for amateur riders, and from 80 to 180 miles for professionals.

But races of this type can be much longer. The Tour de France, the best known of all bicycle races, winds its way for almost 3,000 miles through some of Europe's most rugged terrain. Besides riding ability and great stamina, there is much trickiness involved. Teams work to get one of their members

A road race in New York's Central Park

ahead of the pack, then strive to block opposition riders from challenging the man. Bikes collide; pedals jam spokes. It's a war. And, in the case of the Tour de France, it lasts for more than two weeks.

In track racing, distances are often short, with the 1000-meter race (3,280 feet) being one popular distance. Races are conducted on a steeply banked surface called a velodrome. It can be constructed of wood, clay, asphalt, or concrete.

The racing bike is ultralight, with low handlebars and a high saddle. There are no gears and no

America's Sheila Young won international fame as sprint cyclist.

brakes. You stop by pedaling backwards and grasping the front wheel with one (gloved) hand.

A sprint features a great deal of tricky maneuver-

ing as each rider seeks to get an advantageous position for the final burst to the finish line. Sometimes only inches separate the winner and runner-up.

Track events also include time trials and pursuits. A time trial pits individual riders, not against one another, but against the clock. Pursuit races match rider vs. rider, or team vs. team.

Cycling competition in the United States is supervised by the United States Cycling Federation, and in Canada by the Canadian Cycling Association. These organizations will provide you names and addresses of your local racing associations.

BMX BIKING—The newest kind of bicycling, BMX, involves riding or racing on a sturdy, lightweight pared-down bicycle.

The term BMX is an abbreviation for bicycle motocross, and comes from conventional motocross in which adult competitors race lightweight motorcycles over a cross-country course. (The term motocross is derived from "motorcycle" and "cross-country.")

BMX riding dates to the late 1960s when boys and girls in California began to mimic motorcycle daredevils by racing their bikes on vacant lots and gentle hills where they lived. Little by little, the sport increased in popularity. It got a big boost in 1982 with the release of the movie *E.T., The Extra-Terrestrial*, which featured several young actors riding BMX bikes. About three million boys and girls now own BMX bikes, according to the Bicycle Manufacturers Association.

Tough and sturdy, BMX bikes are also light in weight.

There are more than 700 BMX tracks in operation, ranging from 600 feet to 1,400 feet in length. Most are outdoor courses, but some are well-constructed enclosed structures.

Each race is a sprint, lasting about 50 seconds. Speeds exceed 30 miles per hour.

Tens of thousands of boys and girls compete regularly in BMX races. They are classified by age, sex, and degree of skill—beginner, novice, expert, and pro. Age classifications begin at six-and-under and go to 17-and-over. Prizes are usually trophies or bike shop gift certificates.

Of course, not all BMX riding is competitive

riding. Hundreds of thousands of youngsters ride BMX bikes for fun, bouncing over curbs or performing "wheelies," that is, riding on the rear wheel alone while pulling up on the front of the bike.

Just goofing around has led to another branch of the sport—freestyle BMX, or trick riding. Freestyling enthusiasts often build ramps in their backyards that enable them to indulge in rollbacks, kickturns, aerials, and other such tricks.

How can you find out about BMX activity in your area? Check at a local bike shop, one that specializes in BMX equipment. Or you can write one or both of the two national organizations that sanction BMX racing—the American Bicycle Association or the National Bicycle League. Their addresses are listed in the back of this book. Ask for the information packet these organizations provide for beginner riders.

BMX races are all sprints, each lasting less than a minute.

This BMXer performs on a home-built ramp.

No matter what type of bicycling you plan to do, the chapters that follow will help you. They give advice on how to pick out a bike and how to equip it. They explain how to pedal efficiently and how to ride safely. They tell you how to take care of your bike and make repairs.

As you learn more about the sport and the opportunities it offers for recreation and competition, you may want to sample some of them. With bicycling, the fun keeps building and building.

KINDS OF BICYCLES

A bicycle, says the dictionary, is a vehicle that consists of a metal frame mounted upon two wheels, one behind the other, and that is propelled by pedals and has handlebars for steering. That seems simple enough—until you visit a bike shop. The enormous variety of bicycle models and styles can't help but bewilder you. This chapter explains the different kinds of bicycles that you're likely to come upon.

Array of bikes can make selection difficult.

THE AMERICAN RAMBLER.
FOR LADIES OR GENTLEMEN.

HIGHEST GRADE MADE.

Has Hinged Rear Fork and Spring Frame—the only successful means of preventing vibration—a point which cannot be overestimated.

Price, $125.00.

AMERICAN IDEAL RAMBLER.
FOR BOYS, GIRLS AND LADIES WEIGHING LESS THAN 125 LBS.

Also has Spring Frame, and most of the features embodied in the larger Rambler.

Price, $65.00.

Every Wheel Thoroughly Guaranteed.

Typical bikes of the 1880s

Before you attempt to make a choice, you should understand how a bicycle works. Think of the bike as a machine that converts the vertical energy you create with the up-and-down movement of your legs into horizontal energy—the movement of the bike over the road.

The way in which this is done is not difficult to understand. When you, the rider, push down on the pedals, they turn a toothed wheel called a sprocket or chainwheel. The chain that fits over the chainwheel's metal teeth extends to a smaller sprocket at the rear wheel of the bicycle that is called a freewheel. The moving chain turns both the freewheel and the rear wheel.

What's said above, however, does nothing to explain the most popular feature of modern bikes—multispeed shifting. The multispeed bike has gears that make pedaling easier at certain times. Suppose you're riding along and you come to a steep hill. You shift into a lower gear; you zip up the hill without slowing down. (Chapter 3 explains gear systems in detail.)

Multispeed bikes are classified by the number of gears they have. The principal classifications are 3-speed, 5-speed, 10-speed, 12-speed, and 15-speed.

Bicycles also offer one of two different braking systems—coaster brakes or caliper brakes. In the case of coaster brakes, you stop by pushing backwards on the pedals. With a bicycle that has caliper brakes, you squeeze two levers on the handlebars to stop. The levers act to pull a pair of cables through rubber or plastic tubing, and the cables pinch together two arms, called yokes. Rubber brake shoes attached to the yokes press against the sides of the wheel rim, stopping the wheel's movement. Caliper brakes are also called hand brakes.

Braking and gearing aren't the only variables

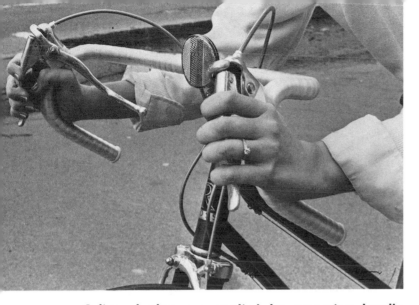

Caliper brakes are applied by squeezing handle levers; that causes rubber brake shoes to press against side of wheel rim.

that bicycles have. There are different wheel and frame sizes and weights, different kinds of handlebars, pedals, and saddles.

What all of this means is that it is possible to pick out a bike today that suits your needs perfectly. All you have to do is pinpoint those needs. Ask yourself these questions: How often are you going to be riding? Will you be doing your riding in the city or the suburbs or in a rural setting? Are you going to be making short trips or long ones? Is hilly terrain going to be a problem?

The amount of experience you've had as a cyclist is another important factor. If you're just starting out, you might want to get a low- or medium-priced bike. Later, when you've gained skill and experience, you can move up to a fancier, lightweight model.

Here is a rundown of the different types of bicycles available:

10-SPEED LIGHTWEIGHT—This is everyone's favorite (and the type of bike this book focuses upon). It provides efficient travel everywhere. It is very light in weight, averaging from 18 to 23 pounds. To keep weight at a minimum, there are no extras—no fenders or chainguard, no kickstand or carriers of any kind. The 10-speed lightweight is meant for riding. Period.

This bike provides great speed with little effort thanks to a clever gear system called the *derailleur*, a French word meaning "derail-er," which partly explains how it works. A 10-speed bike has two gear

15

The 10-speed bike is the type preferred by most cyclists.

The 10-speed bike has two gear sprockets in the front and five at the rear.

sprockets at the front and five at the rear. When you shift (by moving levers that are mounted on the handlebars or frame), you switch the drive chain—you "derail" it, actually—from one sprocket to the next.

The ability to use two different gears in front in combination with five different gears at the rear provides the ten different speeds (2 x 5 = 10).

Generally speaking, the lower gears are for hilly terrain. Medium gears are for riding on level ground. High gears are for high-speed riding.

Lightweight bicycles can be equipped with either raised handlebars or the classic downswept variety. They have caliper brakes and 1½-inch tires on rims of extra-light construction.

Not only are lightweight bikes efficient, they are also versatile. You can use one for running errands, traveling to and from school, for day-long trips, overnight camping, or even race competition.

Such bicycles can be expensive, however, costing anywhere from $200 to more than ten times that amount. (Chapter 4 of this book gives more information on 10-speed bikes.)

There are also 12-speed and 15-speed derailleurs. On a 12-speed derailleur, there are three sprockets in front and four in back, which gives a total of twelve gears (3 x 4 = 12). On the 15-speed bike, there are three sprockets in front and five in back, giving fifteen speeds (3 x 5 = 15).

During the early 1980s, 12-speed bikes spurted in popularity. Many people felt that the convenience

In the 3-speed middleweight, gear system is enclosed within rear hub.

of the two additional gears was worth the added expense.

A 15-speed bike is worth considering if you plan to do a great deal of touring over rough terrain. Such a bike is slightly heavier than the 10-speed bike, and the gear system, being a bit more complex, requires more attention.

3-SPEED MIDDLEWEIGHT—Many people used to refer to these bikes as English racers, which wasn't correct. They're made in the United States and many other countries besides England, and they're not light enough for competitive cycling, weighing

17

from 35 to 45 pounds. What they are good for is day-to-day city riding or short trips.

The 3-speed bike does not have a derailleur gear system. Instead, the gears are housed in the rear axle, or hub. To shift, you stop pedaling and then move a lever on the handlebars to one of three numbers that indicate gears from low to high.

Such bikes have hand brakes and 1⅜- or 1½-inch tires. They get high marks for durability and they don't require much in the way of maintenance. They cost from $150 to $250.

There are also 5-speed middleweights. Some 5-speed bikes have internal hub gears, like the 3-speed bike; others have derailleurs.

To many people, the 5-speed bike does not offer any real advantage over the 3-speed. Yet the 5-speed usually costs more and, if derailleur equipped, can require greater care.

CRUISERS—There are 1-speed bikes, available in a wide range of sizes and styles, from children's sidewalk bicycles with removable training wheels, to sturdy adult models. Sometimes called "paperboy bicycles," cruisers are built entirely of steel tubing, have 2-inch tires, or so-called "balloon" tires, and coaster brakes, brakes that are activated by putting back pressure on the pedals. Cruisers also have what are known as flat handlebars; they're upright, not turned down. Reflectors and kickstands are standard equipment.

Cruisers are fine for short jaunts or running errands. But they're relatively heavy, and you

Cruisers are often used as delivery bikes.

wouldn't enjoy making a long trip over hilly terrain aboard one.

But their lack of comfort is balanced by their ruggedness. They don't require much care and often manage to survive long periods of rough treatment.

BMX BICYCLES—The late 1970s and early 1980s were a period of surging growth for BMX bicycles. During that period, about 40 percent of all bicycles sold in the United States were of the BMX type.

18

(BMX is an abbreviation for bicycle motocross, while the term "motocross" comes from "motorcycle" and "cross-country." A true motocross is a cross-country motorcycle race.)

The BMX bike is a sophisticated machine. Its sturdy, lightweight diamond-shaped frame, usually made of chrome-moly tubing, makes for both speed and durability. For racing competition, 36-spoke wheels with aluminum alloy rims are common, although in recent years "mag" wheels have begun to find favor. These are spokeless wheels that are molded of magnesium or tough thermoplastic. Twenty-inch wheels are the BMX standard.

BMX bikes are fitted with racing saddles and caliper brakes, that is, brakes operated by handlebar-mounted levers. (For more information about BMX, read *Better BMX Riding and Racing for Boys and Girls*, a new title in this series.)

OTHER BICYCLES—Folding bicycles make carrying and storing much easier. They're manufactured in 16-inch, 20-inch, and 24-inch sizes. With most models, the bike folds in two lengthwise by means of a sturdy hinge at mid-frame.

BMX bikes are great for doing wheelies.

Hinge at mid-frame puts the fold in a folding bike.

Tandems, bicycles built for two or even three, are increasing in popularity. They're enjoyable for short rides, but because they're heavier than other types, they're not noted for their speed or efficiency, even though more than one person is pedaling. They're also somewhat difficult to steer. Tandems are now available in both 5-speed and 10-speed styles, as well as the traditional 1-speed, coaster-brake models.

Tandems are now available in 5- and 10-speed styles.

Practice—that's what it takes to become skilled in riding a unicycle.

The unicycle, the one-wheel bike that is steered by shifting one's balance, is still thought by many to be suited only for circus acrobats. But a boy or girl who is willing to practice can learn to ride a unicycle capably and confidently. Both 20-inch and 24-inch models are available.

No matter which kind of bike you're interested in, it's best to stop at a bike shop rather than at a department or discount store. A bike shop dealer will be able to answer whatever questions you might have and also offer the facilities to service or repair your bike should any problems develop.

ALL ABOUT GEARS

One of the chief reasons for cycling's enormous popularity is the variable gear system with which lightweight bicycles are equipped. These have taken the pain out of pedaling, even when you happen to be confronted by a steep hill or cruel headwind.

On a 10-speed bike, you have ten gear choices. Each moves the bike forward at a different rate of speed for a given amount of pedal power.

It is important to understand this gearing system. Unless you do, you won't be able to use your bike the way it was intended to be used.

The principal of gearing is easy to understand if you think of gears in terms of cranks of different

Multispeed bikes have made hill climbing easier.

Most riders prefer gear levers to be mounted on the down tube.

sizes. The longer the handle of the crank, the easier it is to turn, but the greater the distance your hand has to move. It's the same with gears. When the chain of a 10-speed bike is on one of the large sprockets—on one of the low gears—it takes less effort to turn the sprocket, but you have to pedal a greater distance.

Two levers operate the bike's gears. They control cables that extend to the front and rear derailleurs.

21

Levers can also be mounted on the head tube.

There are two different types of controls. The type attached to the bicycle frame is the most common. On the other type, the levers are mounted near the head tube.

Which type is best? It is largely a matter of personal preference.

Two sets of toothed wheels, called sprockets, are the heart of the derailleur system. The first set, located at the pedals, consists of two sprockets. The second, found at the hub of the rear wheel, is made up of five sprockets.

When talking gearing, cyclists refer to the front sprockets as the chainwheel. The sprocket cluster at the rear wheel is known as the freewheel. It may help you to avoid getting the terms mixed up if you remember they are installed in alphabetical order, with the chainwheel (c) before the freewheel (f).

The size of each sprocket is measured, not by its diameter, but by the number of teeth each has. Ask a cyclist the size of a particular sprocket, and he or she will say, for example, "It has 29 teeth."

Not all 10-speed bikes have gears of the same size. They differ as to gear ratios, a term you will hear often (and that is explained later in this chapter).

Bicycle gear ratios range from 28 to 105. The particular ratio of a gear indicates the kind of use it has:

• 28 gear (ratio) to 35 gear (ratio). These are very low gears, requiring a "low" amount of pedaling effort. They are meant for steep hills or traveling over hilly terrain with a heavily loaded bicycle.

• 36 gear to 44 gear; for uphill riding.

• 45 gear to 60 gear; for gentle uphill grades, riding into the wind, or when riding a heavily loaded bicycle on level ground.

• 61 to 85 gear; for riding on level ground. (You'll probably use gears within this range more often than any others.)

• 86 to 105 gear; for high-speed cycling or when traveling downhill. Very high gears require a "high" amount of pedaling effort; they're very tough to push.

What determines gear ratio? The number of teeth on the front sprocket divided by the number of teeth on the rear sprocket, with the result multiplied by the diameter of the bike's wheels. Here is that sentence expressed as a formula:

$$\frac{\text{teeth in front sprocket}}{\text{teeth in back sprocket}} \times \text{wheel diameter} = \text{gear ratio}$$

Suppose you have a 10-speed bicycle whose rear sprockets have 28, 25, 20, 17, and 14 teeth. The front sprockets have 50 and 40 teeth. The bike has 27-inch wheels. On one setting, you use 50 teeth on the front sprocket and 25 teeth on the rear sprocket.

The first number is divided by the second. The result—2—is then multiplied by the diameter of the bike's wheels. The result is a gear ratio of 54.

Doing all of the dividing and multiplying necessary to find all of the gear ratios for a 10-speed bike would be something of a chore. Fortunately, there are charts that enable you to find gear ratios quickly. All you have to do is count the number of teeth in each of the bike's sprockets. One such chart (for bicycles manufactured by the Schwinn Company) appears on this page.

TEETH IN FRONT SPROCKET

TEETH IN REAR SPROCKET	39	40	42	44	45	46	47	48	49	50	51	52
14	75.2	77.1	81.0	84.8	86.8	88.7	90.6	92.6	94.5	96.4	98.3	100.0
	19'8"	20'2"	21'2"	22'2"	22'9"	23'3"	23'9"	24'3"	24'9"	25'3"	25'9"	26'2"
15	70.2	72.0	75.6	79.2	81.0	82.8	84.6	86.4	88.2	90.0	91.8	93.6
	18'5"	18'10"	19'10"	20'9"	21'2"	21'8"	22'2"	22'7"	23'1"	23'7"	24'0"	24'6"
16	65.8	67.5	70.9	74.2	75.9	77.2	79.3	81.0	82.7	84.4	86.1	87.7
	17'3"	17'8"	18'7"	19'5"	19'10"	20'3"	20'9"	21'3"	21'8"	22'1"	22'6"	23'0"
17	61.9	63.5	66.7	69.9	71.4	73.0	74.6	76.2	77.8	79.4	81.0	82.6
	16'2"	16'7"	17'6"	18'4"	18'8"	19'1"	19'6"	19'11"	20'4"	20'9"	21'2"	21'7"
18	58.5	60.0	63.0	66.0	67.5	69.0	70.5	72.0	73.5	75.0	76.5	78.0
	15'4"	15'8"	16'6"	17'3"	17'8"	18'1"	18'5"	18'10"	19'3"	19'1"	20'0"	20'5"
19	55.4	56.8	59.7	62.5	63.9	65.4	66.8	68.2	69.6	71.0	72.4	73.9
	14'6"	14'10"	15'8"	16'4"	16'9"	17'1"	17'6"	17'10"	18'3"	18'7"	18'11"	19'4"
20	52.7	54.0	56.7	59.4	60.7	62.1	63.4	64.8	66.1	67.5	68.8	70.2
	13'10"	14'2"	14'10"	15'7"	15'11"	16'3"	16'7"	17'0"	17'4"	17'8"	18'0"	18'5"
21	50.1	51.4	54.0	56.6	57.8	59.1	60.4	61.7	63.0	64.3	65.5	66.8
	13'1"	13'5"	14'2"	14'10"	15'2"	15'6"	15'10"	16'2"	16'6"	16'10"	17'2"	17'6"
22	47.9	49.1	51.5	54.0	55.2	56.4	57.7	58.9	60.1	61.4	62.5	63.8
	12'6"	12'10"	13'6"	14'2"	14'5"	14'9"	15'1"	15'5"	15'9"	16'1"	16'4"	16'8"
23	45.8	47.0	49.3	51.6	52.8	54.0	55.2	56.3	57.5	58.7	59.8	61.0
	12'0"	12'4"	12'11"	13'6"	13'10"	14'2"	14'5"	14'9"	15'1"	15'4"	15'8"	16'0"
24	43.9	45.0	47.2	49.5	50.6	51.7	52.9	54.0	55.1	56.2	57.3	58.5
	11'6"	11'9"	12'4"	13'0"	13'3"	13'6"	13'10"	14'2"	14'5"	15'0"	15'4"	15'4"
25	42.1	43.2	45.4	47.5	48.6	49.7	50.8	51.8	52.9	54.0	55.1	56.2
	11'0"	11'4"	11'11"	12'5"	12'9"	13'0"	13'4"	13'7"	13'10"	14'2"	14'5"	14'9"
26	40.5	41.5	43.6	45.7	46.7	47.8	48.8	49.8	50.9	51.9	52.9	54.0
	10'7"	10'10"	11'5"	12'0"	12'3"	12'6"	12'9"	13'0"	13'4"	13'7"	13'10"	14'2"
28	37.6	38.5	40.5	42.7	43.3	44.3	45.3	46.3	47.2	48.2	49.2	50.2
	9'10"	10'1"	10'7"	11'2"	11'4"	11'7"	11'10"	12'1"	12'4"	12'7"	12'11"	13'2"

Use this chart to find gear ratios in inches. First, count the number of teeth in the front and rear sprockets of your bike. Then read the lines for each pair of sprockets in which you're interested. Suppose you have a front sprocket with 50 teeth and a rear sprocket with 20 teeth. The gear ratio is 67.5. The figure beneath the 67.5 is the distance covered in feet and inches in one revolution of the pedals—17' 8" in this example.

What's said above is important because when you're picking out a bike you have to be sure you choose one whose gear system is suited for your athletic ability, your experience as a cyclist, as well as the terrain over which you're going to be riding. For example, if you haven't ridden long distances very often, are not built like a football linebacker, and do not expect to have to ascend steep hills, there wouldn't be any reason to have any gears on your bicycle above 90, maybe even above 85 or 80. A gear of, say, 102, would be a complete waste. You wouldn't even be able to turn the pedals.

On the other hand, if you happen to be an experienced cyclist, and do happen to be built like a linebacker, you would want gears in the low ranges, less than 40, say. Otherwise, you'd pedal like crazy but you'd never move very far.

Generally speaking, as a beginner rider, you will want a wide range of gear ratios, from the 30s through the 90s. You might have two low gears (in the 30s and 40s) and two high gears (in the 80s and 90s), and the others in the middle ranges.

An experienced cyclist does not require so wide a range. A racing bicycle, for instance, might have gear ratios that range from the mid-50s to 100.

Be sure to discuss gears and their ratios with the dealer when you go to purchase your 10-speed bike. The efficiency with which you ride—and your enjoyment—depend on getting gears of the right size.

Modern bicycle frames boast both strength and lightness.

BIKES AND THEIR PARTS

The gear system is only one of many different topics you should consider when buying a multi-speed bike. Here are some others:

THE FRAME—The frame, the heart of the bike, is the rigid metal structure on which all the parts fit. The more you pay for a frame, the less it is going to weigh but without any loss of strength.

In a cheap bike, the frame is made of seamed tubing. It is relatively heavy, not particularly strong, and has no "give" to it. Pedaling over a rough surface can make for an unpleasant ride.

With better bikes, the frames are made of seamless tubing which is lighter in weight and stronger. The very best bikes usually have frames of the

Tube joint above is lugged; joint below isn't.

lightest and strongest steel alloys—manganese molybdenum or chrome molybdenum.

The method by which the frame parts are joined is also important. The cheapest method is to simply stick two tubes together and then weld them. Such joints aren't very strong. While you are not likely to have any problem in ordinary use, if you try curb-hopping or otherwise abuse the bike, a joint of this type can split.

In better bikes, the frame tubes are lugged and brazed, not merely welded. Lugging involves the use of a metal sleeve at the joint, which strengthens it. Brazing, like welding, is a process of joining two pieces of metal, but brazing is done at a lower temperature than welding, and thus it weakens the metal only slightly.

In a high-quality frame, the tubes are butted. This means the tube walls are slightly thicker at the ends. Butting means added strength where the tubes join. How can you tell when a frame is con-

Butted tube (top) is thickset at end, where most strength is needed.

Brakes can be side pull (right) or center pull.

It's claimed that center-pull brakes are more reliable because they're better balanced. They don't require as much adjusting, either. But very expensive side-pulls are sometimes found on bikes of the very highest quality.

TIRES—Most 10-speed bikes ride on clincher tires. The clincher is preferred because it has a separate tube which fits inside the tire. The open edges of the clincher have a wire or "bead" running inside the tire edge. The bead holds a tire in place on the rim.

Sew-ups are a second type of tire. With sew-ups, the tube is actually sewn into the tire.

Some riders choose sew-ups because they are lighter in weight than clinchers. Indeed, a sew-up and its rim can weigh about half as much as a clincher and its rim. Sew-ups are also narrower. With less tire surface in contact with the road, you move faster and with greater overall ease.

The disadvantage of sew-ups becomes apparent when you get a flat and have to make repairs. You just can't do it on the road—unless you have taken the trouble of carrying a spare tire with you which, of course, can be a bother.

Clinchers, on the other hand, are easier to repair on the road. All you need is a patch kit and a pump. Another advantage of clinchers is that they cost considerably less than sew-ups.

HANDLEBARS—Dropped bars or flat bars? That's the decision you have to make. Dropped bars are the downswept kind. They're extremely popular

structed of butted tubes? Look for a decal on the frame that says so.

BRAKES—Hand-operated caliper brakes are common to virtually all 10-speed bikes. The pulling power you generate when you squeeze the handlebar levers causes the rubber brake shoes to press against the wheel rims, and this brings the wheel to a stop.

Brakes are mechanically designed so that the pulling power is exerted from either the center or the side. Most lower-priced 10-speed bikes have side-pull brakes, while center-pulls are usually found on the better bikes.

Clincher (above) is much more popular than sew-up.

supported by both your hands and your seat, bumps in the road are much easier to take.

Another advantage is that dropped bars provide for several different hand positions. Riding with the hands close to the brake levers is the "normal" position; it makes for efficient pedaling and quick braking.

When heading up a long hill, grip the bars near

Dropped bars permit several different hand positions. Riding with hands close to brake levers (above) is considered "normal" position. When heading uphill, grip at handle ends.

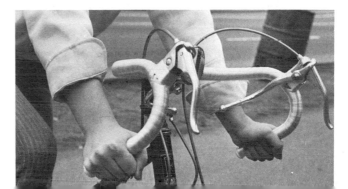

nowadays. Flat bars have no sweep.

There are several reasons that the majority of young riders prefer dropped bars. When you're pedaling along with a bike that is so equipped, you lean forward and stretch out your spine. Your breathing capacity is increased. Since your weight is

the handle ends. This helps to get your arm, shoulder, and back muscles involved in the task. And since you're bent over more, wind resistance is less.

In a third position, you grip with your hands side by side, divided only by the handlebar stem. This style permits you to be more upright in the seat. You can look around, do some sight-seeing.

With flat bars, you ride stiff-spined. You tend to feel the bumps more.

With hands together, divided only by handlebar stem, you can ride more upright.

Flat bars give greater steering control.

Flat bars, however, do give you greater steering control and more maneuverability. And since your chin is up, you have a better view of the road ahead.

So, which should it be, flat or dropped? One rule of thumb says that if your normal biking trip is 20 miles or longer, choose dropped bars. They make for smooth sailing. (If you do select dropped bars, don't do as some young riders do and turn them backwards, so the handle ends point forward or even skyward. This cuts your ability to turn and maneuver; it's very hazardous.) If you seldom make extended trips, flat bars are probably better for you.

No decision is absolutely final. If you pick the dropped style, but decide after a few weeks you're simply not comfortable with them, you can switch

to the flat type. Just remember, you have to change brake levels, too.

SADDLE—If you've chosen dropped bars, then you'll also want to pick out a racing saddle. Long, narrow, and unpadded, the racing saddle minimizes friction between the legs and makes pedaling easier.

With flat bars, choose a mattress saddle. The mattress saddle is wider and has metal springs.

The best racing saddles are made of leather. It takes about 500 miles of riding to get a leather saddle properly broken in, but once this is accomplished, you'll love it because it will be so comfortable.

A plastic saddle does not require any breaking in. It also can withstand ill treatment better. For example, you can leave a plastic saddle out in the rain without doing damage to it, but don't try that with the leather.

If you have some extra money, splurge on a saddle. You're going to be spending many hours in your saddle, so what you're actually buying is comfort.

Don't, however, confuse comfort with saddle softness. By their nature, saddles are hard. When you pedal, the saddle has to be able to resist the force created by your feet and legs. A soft saddle would dissipate this power. Even a mattress saddle shouldn't be too springy.

RIMS AND HUBS—Better bikes are equipped with wheel rims of aluminum alloy, while less costly bikes have steel rims. Not only are aluminum rims better

A racing saddle (above) with a sew-up lashed to it, and a mattress saddle.

Rims are available in an enormous variety of sizes and styles.

because they're lighter, but they offer a surer braking surface in wet weather.

Each wheel has a hub at its center, a cylinder-shaped unit that has been machined to hold the axle and bearings and drilled to receive the spokes. Hubs, like rims, are available in aluminum alloy or steel.

It's worthwhile to buy a bike that has quick-release hubs. These enable you to remove a wheel by flipping a pair of levers. The alternative, of course, is tackling a pair of bolts with a wrench.

The quick-release feature is desirable should you have to store your bike in a small space, such as a closet, transport it inside an automobile, or leave it locked in the street (in which case you should remove one wheel and lock it next to the frame and other wheel or take it with you).

PEDALS—Pedals come with either sealed bearings or adjustable bearings (or, in the case of cheap pedals, with no ball bearings at all). Choose sealed bearings. They're the best.

30

Let's suppose you've completed your tour of the bike shop, and you've appraised the different kinds of pedals, saddles, handlebars, and other parts. In each case, let's further suppose you've made a choice. But you're still not ready to put your money down, hop aboard, and ride away. You have to first make sure the bike is going to fit you properly. Getting fitted is the subject of the next chapter.

Lever at hub is a tip-off that this is a "quick-release" hub.

Measuring the seat tube, which extends from the seat to the bottom bracket

GETTING A BIKE THAT FITS

Once you've decided on the kind of bike you want, the next step is to get fitted. Unless your bike is the right size for you, you'll never be able to enjoy it to the fullest.

Getting the right fit means buying a bike of the proper frame size. This is determined by measuring the almost vertical tube into which the seat post fits. Called the seat tube, it extends from the seat

31

to the bottom bracket (the small cylinder at the bottom of the frame into which the crank axle fits). Measure the seat tube from its very top to the center of the bottom bracket.

If the seat tube is 24 inches in length, the bicycle has a 24-inch frame. Frame sizes very from 17 to 26 inches.

What frame size do you require? It depends on the inside length of your leg. To determine this, have someone measure the distance along the inside of your leg from your crotch to the floor. (You should be standing in your stocking feet or cycling shoes.) Once this measurement has been determined, use this chart as a guide to determine the frame size you should buy:

Leg Length	Frame Size
from 26 to 30 inches	17 inches
from 28 to 31 inches	19 inches
from 29 to 32 inches	20 inches
from 30 to 33 inches	21 inches
from 31 to 34 inches	22 inches
from 32 to 35 inches	23 inches
from 33 to 36 inches	24 inches
from 34 to 37 inches	25 inches
from 35 to 38 inches	26 inches

Once you have picked out a bike of the right frame size, check the fit with this test. Stand in your stocking feet or cycling shoes, and straddle the top tube (the horizontal tube that extends from the handlebars to the seat). There should be some

When you straddle the top tube, it should almost touch your body.

space between your body and the top of the tube. How much space depends to some degree upon your height. If you're a bit shorter than average, there should be hardly any space at all. You may even be touching the top tube. A taller than average person requires a little more space, anywhere from ¾ to 1 inch.

"GIRLS' BIKES"—In years past, there was a clear-cut distinction between bikes for boys and bikes for girls. A boy's bike had a top tube (sometimes called a "gender bar") while a girl's bike didn't (so as to accommodate skirts). Instead of a top tube, the girl's bike had a tube that slanted downward from the head tube to the seat tube, running almost parallel to the down tube.

A boy or girl of the 1940s or 1950s would never even think of riding a bike manufactured for the opposite sex. To do so was almost scandalous.

It's different today. Younger women have no hesitation about buying and riding bikes with boys' frames, or what has come to be called a "normal" frame by some manufacturers.

The truth is that girls have little choice in the matter. Bicycle manufacturers no longer offer every bike size in both boys' and girls' models, only boys'. Indeed, only the 19-inch and 21-inch frame sizes are likely to be available with girls' frames. No racing bikes at all are manufactured in girls' models. While bikes with girls' frames may not yet have gone the way of pet rocks and skateboard parks, it could happen.

MIXTE FRAMES—To replace the conventional girl's frame, many manufacturers now offer mixte frames. Sometimes called the unisex frame, the mixte is superior to the standard girl's frame because it is much stronger. Instead of a top tube, it features a pair of metal struts that extend from the headset to the rear hub, giving three points of attachment rather than merely two as in traditional open-frame bikes.

Traditional girl's bike has no top tube.

Mixte frame features pair of metal struts that extend from headset to rear hub.

Mixte frames are becoming available in more and more styles and models. Some observers say the mixte is the bike of the future.

ADJUSTING THE SEAT—Let's suppose you've decided on a bike whose style appeals to you and has a frame of the proper size. The next step is to adjust the height of the saddle.

Many riders have their saddles set too low. You can't generate all the pedaling power of which you're capable if the saddle is too low, because you're unable to get full use of your thigh muscles.

34

A rule of thumb that most expert riders obey says that your saddle is at the right level when you can sit on your bike with your heel on the pedal while it is at the lowest point, and you are able to straighten your leg. This means that when you are pedaling with the ball of your foot on the pedal, your leg will be almost fully extended at the bottom of each stroke. This assures the greatest amount of pedaling power.

Once you get the saddle height adjusted, don't be upset if it doesn't feel right at first. Give it a fair try. If you ride a 100 miles or so with the seat at the recommended level, and it still feels uncomfortable, then make whatever other adjustments

When you're seated on the bike and pedaling, your leg should be straight when pedal reaches lowest point.

you feel are necessary. Bike comfort is more important than pedaling efficiency.

You may also want to tinker with the tilt of the saddle in your search for comfort. Most experts recommend the saddle be kept perfectly level, although a tiny amount of forward tilt might possibly contribute to your comfort. A back-tilted saddle, however, is very rare.

There is one other saddle adjustment you should make, sliding it backward or forward so it is properly lined up with the pedals. Here's the formula to follow: Sit on the saddle with the balls of your feet on the pedals, then rotate the pedals until they are both the same distance from the ground. At that point, the saddle is properly adjusted if the knee of your forward leg is directly over the center of the forward pedal.

ADJUSTING THE HANDLEBARS—Once you're finished with the saddle, adjust the handlebars. Line them up so the top of the handlebars is at the same level as the nose, or front, of the seat.

EQUIPMENT AND ACCESSORIES

Shop carefully for any extras you may require, especially those items of equipment that have to do with safety. According to a study by *Consumer Guide*, many bicycle accessories should be classified as mere toys. They lack in both reliability and durability. Always look for quality.

CARRIERS—There is a tremendous variety of carriers to choose from. The type you select depends upon your needs, that is, how much you have to carry.

The smallest carriers are nylon bags that strap to the rear of the saddle or to the handlebars. Also

Bike carriers can be used to tote almost any kind of light load.

popular are lightweight aluminum-alloy racks that fit over the rear wheel and attach to the brake center bolt. You can then strap gear to the rack or mount a box atop it.

The food and equipment you require for long trips demand panniers. These are good-sized bags,

Rear panniers are the most efficient way of carrying something.

Most cyclists prefer to lean bikes than rely on kickstands.

made of canvas or waterproof nylon, that hang alongside the wheels on special racks. Not only do panniers carry gear efficiently, but their low center of gravity adds to stability.

There are both front panniers and rear panniers. Rear panniers are the best. Front panniers make for difficult steering and do not have quite the carrying capacity of rear panniers.

KICKSTAND—If you're going to be making frequent long trips with your bike, you probably will come to realize that you don't need a kickstand. It adds a good deal of weight without fulfilling any vital use. You can always lean the bike against something.

PUMP—A cylinder-shaped pump for fixing flats on the road is vital. Such pumps are not expensive, costing only about $15. They clip easily to the

Bell and speedometer are not considered necessities.

A hand pump is a critical piece of equipment on any long trip.

bicycle frame. Some are equipped with a handy air-pressure gauge.

BELLS AND HORNS—If you're a city rider, a small bell or horn that attaches to the handlebars to alert pedestrians of your approach seems like a good idea. But wait—bells and horns have a habit of failing at the moment they are most needed. They also get stolen frequently. Why not simply imitate the sound of a bell or horn whenever a pedestrian strays into your path? Go "Ding! Ding!" or "Beep! Beep!" Try it; it works!

SPEEDOMETER—Few serious bikers bother with speedometers. Most models are not reliable and, since they're driven by the front wheel, they increase drag. On a long trip, the drag can become very noticeable.

ODOMETER—From the Greek word *hodos*, which means road, and *metron*, meaning measure, the

Odometer keeps track of miles you travel.

thing like the rearview mirror in a family automobile. In size, they more resemble the small, circular mirror the dentist uses to get a look deep inside your mouth.

One type of bicycle rearview mirror mounts atop the hood that shields the brake lever; another type attaches to the visor of your helmet. A third type is worn at the wrist. Each kind requires a good deal of practice before worthwhile results begin to be achieved. Even then, your field of vision is quite limited. Rearview mirrors are best classified as "gimmicks."

odometer is a small device that keeps track of the miles you travel. Bicycle shops sometimes call them cyclometers or velometers.

This instrument, which is about the size of a small matchbox, is mounted on the front fork. A small pick is then attached to one of the front spokes. The pick turns the odometer wheel and thereby registers the distance traveled.

One problem with the odometer is the sound it creates. Every time the pick engages the odometer wheel the spoke gives off a twanging sound. On a long trip, this can become very bothersome.

What's the solution? Forget the odometer altogether. Figure out the miles you plan to travel or have traveled by consulting a road map.

REARVIEW MIRRORS—Yes, there are rearview mirrors for bicycles. They are not, however, any-

One type of rearview mirror attaches to helmet visor.

Small generator like this can be used to power lights.

Right: Hub-mounted, battery-powered light

LIGHTS—If you intend to do any riding after dark, buy lights—a white light at the front, a red light for the rear.

There are two basic types of lights: the battery light and the kind that operates off a small generator. Unfortunately, both types are a long way from perfection.

Battery lights mount on the handlebars. They are relatively heavy and easily stolen when you park and leave the bike. Being battery powered, the beam is strong when the light is working on fresh batteries, but it gradually fades.

One way to solve the last-named problem is to purchase a rechargeable battery light. When you're not using it, you plug it into a household electrical outlet, and the battery automatically recharges. When touring, you will find that the battery unit and recharging attachment are relatively heavy. Another drawback is that you may not have a recharging source.

Should you require a light only once in a while, consider mounting a clamp that holds an ordinary flashlight in position on your handlebars. Then, when you must ride at night, you simply insert a flashlight in the clamp.

With the generator system, a small generator

Water bottle can be carried on bike frame.

attaches to the front fork and takes power off of the front wheel. As long as you're moving along at a good speed, the light is bright. But when you slow down and stop, it quickly fades. Also, the small wheel of the generator creates drag. But with a generator system, you get a certain satisfaction out

of creating your own energy supply and being freed from dependence on Eveready.

WATER BOTTLE—Carried on the bike frame, a water bottle enables you to tote your own supply of liquid, be it water or fruit juice. Health experts say that you should drink three or four times an hour when cycling on a hot day.

TOE CLIPS—These serve to clamp each foot to its related pedal, which enables you to pull up on the pedals as well as push down. This boosts pedaling efficiency tremendously. Some experts say that toe clips can actually double your power output. Be sure to get the size that corresponds to your shoe size.

Bicycle shoes and toe clips are worn by all serious cyclists.

If you're using toe clips for the first time, you may find getting underway a bit tricky since it's not possible to strap in both feet in a standing-still position.

Try this technique: Straddle the bike. Then slip your left foot onto the related pedal and tighten the toe-clip strap.

Push off, using the downstroke of your left foot to get you going. Using your right foot, spin the related toe clip around to get it into proper position, and then slip the foot in.

When the right pedal is at the highest point of its arc, reach down with your right hand (do it by feel; don't look down) and tighten the strap. Practice this a few times and it will become easy.

When coming to a stop, reverse the procedure. Slow down, coast. With your right pedal at the 12 o'clock position, reach down and loosen the right toe-clip strap so you can slip the right foot free. When you stop, undo the left strap.

Toe clips can be something of a hazard on city streets or anytime you encounter traffic. Loosen the straps under such conditions. You want to be able to slip your feet off the pedals quickly should an emergency occur.

BICYCLE SHOES—These have a metal or fiberglass shank within the sole that makes for even foot pressure on the pedals. Thus, like toe clips, bike shoes increase pedaling efficiency.

LOCKS—If you intend to keep your bike, you must lock it everytime you leave it unattended,

In locking a bike with a quick-release hub, remove the front wheel and take it with you (or lock it next to the rear wheel).

even if it is only or a minute or so. Use a Kryptonite or Citadel lock. U-shaped and made of high-strength steel (but vinyl-covered to protect your bike's finish), such locks are designed to withstand attacks by hacksaws, prybars, boltcutters, and the like. Mere chains are easy to cut.

Always lock the bike frame and rear wheel to an immovable object—a lamp post or a parking sign imbedded in concrete. Carry the front wheel with you.

Many communities offer bike registration programs through local police departments. When you enroll in such a program, an identifying number is engraved on the frame of your bike and registered with the police department. An Operation I.D. decal is then placed on the bike to help discourage theft. If your bicycle should ever get stolen and is later recovered, the identifying number helps in getting the bike back. Inquire at a local police precinct to find out whether this program is available in your community.

If you're not able to take advantage of a bicycle registration program, you should write down identifying information about your bike and keep it in a safe place for future reference. This information should include the bike's make, model, and serial number, as well as a general description of it.

PEDALING, SHIFTING, BRAKING

Even if you've been a bicycle rider for several years, you may not be using the most efficient pedaling technique. It's called "ankling." The foot pivots at the ankle on each stroke. This enables you to use the big muscles of your legs and thighs in a smooth, continuous flow of power.

Place the ball of the foot on the pedal. Never use the arch or heel when pedaling.

Begin at the top of the stroke—at a 12 o'clock position—with the toes slightly higher than the heel.

Push downward with the ball of the foot, pivoting on the ankle. At between 2 and 3 o'clock, the foot should level out.

Continue pushing. At the bottom of the stroke—6 o'clock—the toes are lower than the heel.

Now the foot begins the upstroke, moving toward the "toes-higher" position it will reach at 12 o'clock.

Practice ankling until you can do it without consciously think about it. Ankling should become as natural as breathing.

SHIFTING—While pedaling is not likely to offer you the slightest problem, shifting gears is another matter. Indeed, beginning riders have more difficulty with shifting than anything else.

The idea of shifting is to keep pedal pressure the same at all times. By so doing, you level out the uphills and downhills, turning the roadway into an endless level strip over which you glide steadily and easily.

The ankling technique of pedaling—with the toes down on the downstroke, heel down on the upstroke.

At the top of the pedaling stroke, toes are down, heel up.

43

Shifting lever on left controls chainwheel.

Before you begin practicing, there are a couple of things to remember. First, never shift a 10-speed bike unless you are pedaling. Otherwise, you can bend or break gear teeth or similarly damage the chain.

Second, the less tension the chain is under when you shift, the better. The easiest time to shift is when you are on level ground. The most difficult time is when you're pedaling uphill. (Actually, you should never be in a position where you have to shift in

the midst of an uphill grade. You should always plan ahead, shifting when you see the hill coming, not when you're halfway up it.)

On a 10-speed bike, the shifting lever on the left controls the chainwheel (front), and the lever on the right controls the freewheel (rear). There are two choices of gears in the front and five in the back.

If you have trouble remembering which lever controls the front and which the back, keep in mind that it's the right one that controls the rear sprocket. It's right, rear; right, rear.

In the case of the chainwheel (front), the small wheel is the lowest gear. With the freewheel (back), the opposite is true—the biggest sprocket is the lowest gear.

When you pull the left lever toward you, you move from a low gear to a high gear. But when you pull the right lever toward you, you move from a higher gear to a lower one.

The first time you try shifting, you'll realize the shift levers do not have stops for the various gears. You have to learn how they move by feel.

When you shift properly, the switchover from one gear to the next is practically noiseless. All you hear is the reassuring "plunk" as the chain eases into the sprocket teeth.

One word of warning: You should never attempt to ride with the chain crossing from the biggest sprocket in the front to the biggest sprocket in the rear, or from the smallest front sprocket to the smallest sprocket in the back. In so doing, you make the chain ride at too sharp an angle, putting it under severe strain. This increases chain wear.

Smooth and efficient shifting depends to a great extent on your ability to plan ahead. If you don't plan ahead, you may find yourself halfway up a steep grade and needing to shift desperately, but unable to do so because the chain is under too much tension.

The solution is to keep your eye on the road far ahead and notice where uphill grades begin. Mark that point by lining it up with a rock, tree, or some other object. When you reach that point, shift. Otherwise, a hill can come upon you almost without your knowing it.

It takes plenty of practice to become skilled in shifting gears. When you're learning to shift, it's a good idea to shift frequently, even when approaching the gentlest of uphill grades. The idea is to try to make shifting as natural as pedaling.

A final word about shifting: Most riders who are new to 10-speed bikes don't take full advantage of the gear system. They gear too high and pedal too slowly. They wear themselves out quickly as a result. It's better to pedal rapidly against little resistance. You'll last much longer.

CADENCE—Keeping a constant pedaling speed is the most efficient way to ride. Experienced riders maintain the same speed over long distances by counting cadence. They pedal with the same number of strokes per minute, counting them off one-by-one.

How many strokes per minute should you establish for yourself? It depends on several factors—your age, size, and physical condition; your experience and skill as a cyclist; and the quality and condition of your bike.

If you're a beginner, you'll probably be comfortable using anywhere from 50 to 75 pedaling strokes per minute. Adult cyclists of long experience often pedal at a rate of as many as 100 strokes per minute. Racers do even more.

One of the functions of your gear system should be to help you maintain your cadence. Shift down and up as necessary, while maintaining the same number of strokes per minute.

BRAKING—The 10-speed bike has hand-operated caliper brakes. In most instances, the left-hand lever controls the brakes at the front wheel, while the right-hand lever controls the brakes at the rear.

Under most conditions, it's best to squeeze both levers with equal pressure at the same time to stop. But each set of brakes has its own stopping characteristics. You should test your brakes by making quick stops at low speeds, then gradually increase your speed. Keep practicing until you're able to make abrupt stops at high speeds without any fear of losing control of the bike.

When you apply both brakes with equal pressure, it's the front brake that does most of the work. Thus, you should be cautious about braking too hard when traveling extremely fast. When the front wheel brakes hard and fast, you can find yourself

45

To stop, it's usually best to squeeze both brake levers with equal pressure.

being pitched over the front handlebars.

Suppose you're speeding downhill and want to stop. The correct braking procedure is to apply and release both sets of brakes several times in quick succession—on-off, on-off, on-off. This technique helps to avoid a pitchover. It is also easier on the brake pads; they're less likely to heat up, which causes undue wear.

It is also a good idea to use the on-off braking technique when the roadway is wet. This helps to remove water from the rims. When the rims are wet, the brake pads have little stopping power.

Favor the rear-wheel brakes (the controls on the right) anytime you encounter slippery conditions. You may skid, but a rear-wheel skid shouldn't send a bike out of control. A front-wheel skid, on the other hand, can be a disaster.

46

BIKE SAFETY

Cycling is one of the safest of all leisure-time activities. Yet statistics reveal that in one recent year about 460,000 people were injured in bicycle accidents seriously enough to require emergency care.

Research concerning bicycle-related accidents have brought to light some interesting findings:

• Most accidents take place on bright, sunny days (because there are more cyclists on the road when the weather is good).

• Most accidents occur on Saturdays. The late afternoon—from 4 o'clock to 6 o'clock—is the most hazardous time of day.

Good advice from a cycling backpacker

Left: **The left arm straight out means a left turn.** *Center:* **The left arm out with the hand extended upward indicates a right turn.** *Right:* **Left hand down indicates a stop.**

- Most accidents occur at intersections that are unequipped with traffic control devices.
- A majority of accidents involve the 12-to-15-year-old age group.

What's tragic about bicycle accidents is that so many of them could have been prevented. According to the National Safety Council, four out of five accidents involving bikes and motor vehicles might never have occurred had the cyclists been observing local traffic regulations.

So, for safe cycling, obey the rules. Here are the most important of them:

Keep to the right side of the road. A rule that you have probably complied with many times states that pedestrians walking on country roads should keep to the left. But when you are mounted on a bicycle, you are no longer a pedestrian; your bicycle is a vehicle and is subject to many of the same rules as an automobile. One of these states that whether you're using a highway or a city street, you must ride on the right side of the road—*with* the traffic.

Ride in a straight line; don't weave in and out. And if you're riding with a friend, don't ride side-by-side; keep in single file.

Make right turns from the right lane and left turns from the left lane.

Use hand signals to indicate turns. The left arm

straight out is the signal for a left turn. The left arm straight out, with the arm bent upward at a 90-degree angle and the hand upstretched, is the signal for a right turn. The left hand pointing downward is a signal that you're going to stop.

Anytime you signal, be sure to do so well before you actually execute the turn. At the time you turn, you want to be sure that you have both hands on the handlebars; one hand should not be involved in signaling.

Obey all signal lights, stop signs, and other traffic regulations just as if you were driving a car.

Slow down at intersections; be extra cautious. The best way to cross a busy intersection is to dismount and walk your bike across in the pedestrian lane. By becoming a pedestrian, you gain a number of rights and privileges that cyclists don't enjoy and your chances of crossing safely are increased immeasurably.

Yield the right-of-way to pedestrians. Don't ride on sidewalks (unless local regulations permit it).

Never carry a passenger. Bikes are made for one rider. With a passenger riding on the top tube, it's difficult to keep the bike under control and your view of the road ahead is obstructed.

Leave your Walkman at home. Safe cycling demands that you use your ears as well as your eyes. A radio blots out sounds that otherwise would serve to warn you. Listening to a radio is something like wearing a blindfold.

Be extra cautious on wet streets. Try to keep your brakes dry by applying them lightly as you ride. After riding through a puddle, bear in mind you may be completely brakeless. Stop; walk your bike until the rims dry.

Walk the bike across busy intersections.

Lights are essential for night riding. A rear light is as vital as a front light, perhaps even more so. It should be capable of throwing a beam that is visible from 500 feet. (For information on different types of lights, see Chapter 6.) Reflectors—both rear and side reflectors—are also important. Reflectors should be at least three inches in diameter and be able to be seen from a distance of 500 feet.

Beware of streets designated as "Bike Routes." Many cities are guilty of establishing bike routes on busy streets. Signs are placed at intervals along these streets that proclaim BIKE ROUTE, and which are meant to alert motorists to the fact that cyclists are using the street. Sometimes a painted stripe indicates a particular lane is intended for bicycles. Don't feel that you are protected when using one of these Bike Routes. Drivers veer in and out of designated bike lanes at will. Vehicles even park in them. Your best bet is to pretend the lane doesn't exist, and ride accordingly.

Don't, however, confuse a "Bike Route" with a "Bike Path." They are very different. The term "Bike Path" refers to a specially constructed route

Beware of official bike routes.

There is a wide range of helmet shapes and styles.

that is completely divorced from city streets or country roads. You can ride along a "Bike Path" and never even see an automobile. But such Bike Paths are expensive to construct, and are thus very much of a rarity.

Wear a helmet. Head injuries are the most serious of all. A helmet can help to protect your head.

The classic cycling helmet is constructed of thick strips of leather that run across the top of the skull. Such helmets offer next to no head protection. Some riders, in fact, now sarcastically refer to helmets of this type as "hair nets."

The modern cycling helmet was developed during the 1970s and early 1980s. In some ways, it resembles a motorcycle helmet (but it does not

49

Helmeted BMX riders await race start.

restrict the rider's vision as some motorcycle helmets do, nor is it as heavy).

When you go to purchase a bicycle helmet, look for these characteristics:

• An outer shell of strong, rigid, lightweight material, such as Lexan.

• An energy-absorbing liner.

• A strap or harness that tightens under the jaw to help hold the helmet in place should an accident occur.

Helmets are available in about as many sizes as hats. Be sure the helmet you buy fits correctly, that it is matched to your head size.

Ride defensively—that's the chief rule you should seek to follow. Always expect the unexpected. When you're riding next to a line of cars parked at the curb, assume that a driver is going to open a door and block your path. When you're approaching an intersection and a car is coming from the opposite direction, take it for granted that it is going to turn to the left and cut across your path. In other words, be prepared for the worst. You'll then have an extra second or two to put on the brakes or do whatever else has to be done to avoid disaster when things go wrong.

BIKE CARE AND REPAIR

Remember how good your bike felt when you rode it for the first time. Well, that's how it should feel all of the time.

Taking good care of your bike is the way to assure smooth, trouble-free operation. This means doing your own repair work and performing maintenance chores.

You don't have to be a certified mechanic to follow the suggestions set down in this chapter. They are all simple tasks that any bike owner should be able to accomplish.

Having your bike perform at its highest level isn't the only benefit you get by doing repairs and maintenance yourself. It also saves you money. If you have had any work performed at a bike shop recently, you know that parts and labor cost a great deal.

You also save time. Toting a bike to the repair shop, discussing its problems with the mechanic, having the repairs done, and then returning to pick up the bike can take a week or more.

Despite what is said above, there are several types of repairs you should never consider doing yourself, not even if you feel you have superior mechanical skills. Don't fool with a loose or bent crank. Don't attempt to true a wheel that's out of alignment. Never attempt to oil or grease sealed bearings. Be wary about taking apart any derailleur system. Problems concerning these parts should be

Checking for loose bolts

dealt with by a professional.

Problems you can solve yourself are discussed on the pages that follow.

TIGHTENING LOOSE NUTS AND BOLTS—Before you take your bike out on the road, check for loose nuts and bolts. Doing so can help to avoid serious problems.

Use a wrench (6-inch or 8-inch adjustable-end) to test for loose nuts on the axles and handlebars. Check the saddle bolt nut and the fender bolts.

Pick the bike up by the saddle and shake it from side to side. Listen for any unusual rattle. It may be a part that needs tightening.

To check for play in the headset, apply the front brake and push the bike forward against the locked wheel. Is there any headset wobble? This test is also

51

a good brake check. Perform the same test with rear brakes and rear fork.

Pick up the front of the bike with one hand by the handlebars, letting the rear wheel rest on the ground, and with the other hand try wiggling the front wheel from side-to-side. If there's play there, the wheel bearings, called cones, may need tightening.

Turn the bike upside down and remove the wheel. Undo the locknuts on each side of the axle that hold the cones in place. With a wrench in each hand, tighten both cones at the same time. It's likely that one is looser than the other, which means you'll have to be turning one a greater distance than the other.

Adjusting the cones is a delicate job. Test the adjustment by replacing the wheel and spinning it. If you've tightened the cones too much, friction will prevent the wheel from spinning freely. If, on the other hand, you have failed to tighten the cones sufficiently, you'll still have some side-to-side play. Getting it right is a trial-and-error process. In the case of a quality wheel and hub which are in perfect adjustment, the wheel's spin is unimpeded to such an extent that the weight of the tire valve pulls the wheel around so the valve comes to rest at a 6 o'clock position.

Give the rear wheel the same test. Pick the bike up by the front of the saddle, allowing its weight to be supported by the front wheel and your hand. Then check for side-to-side wobble. If there is some,

Check air pressure with a gauge.

the rear cones need tightening. Follow the same procedure.

INFLATING TIRES—For easy riding and long mileage, keep your tires inflated at recommended levels. (The correct tire pressure is stamped on the tire sidewalls.) A soft tire can lead to rim or wheel damage, while an overinflated tire can blow out. Keeping the tires at their correct pressure is worth the time it takes.

As this may imply, you should buy an air-pressure gauge. You also should own your own air pump. Hand pumps require more effort, much more effort than a gas station pump when it comes to inflating your tires, but they are much safer.

If you're like most riders, there will be times you will use a gas station pump. Be very careful. Getting air from a gas station pump is something like trying to take a drink of water from a fire hose. You get much more than you actually want, so much more, in fact, it's hazardous. A gas station air pump can blow the tire right off the rim of a 10-speed bike in the blink of an eye.

When you're filling a tire at a gas station pump, don't attempt to do it in one blast. Do it with many short shots, keeping the nozzle tight to the valve for only a second or two at a time. Squeeze the tire between your thumb and forefinger as the air floods in. You should be able to tell by feel when the tire is approaching correct pressure. Check the pressure with your gauge before you ride away.

Incidentally, the pressure that is marked on the side of the tire does not necessarily apply in every case. A person who is lighter than average does not require as much air pressure as is recommended, while a heavier-than-average individual is advised to add a few pounds of pressure.

On extremely hot days, with the temperatures soaring into the 90s, it's wise to reduce air pressure by three or four pounds. Air expands when temperatures rise, increasing the pressure. You reduce the chance of a blowout by underinflating slightly.

Besides being concerned about air pressure you should also inspect the tire treads from time to time for signs of wear. Look for cuts or breaks that indi-cate a new tire is needed. Also be on the lookout for uneven tread wear, a clue that a wheel may be out of line and your brakes need adjusting. When a brake is gripping excessively on one side of the wheel, tread wear on that side becomes apparent.

LUBRICATION—There are many types of bicycle lubricants, but oil is the one you'll be using the most. Do not use ordinary household oil, however, because it attracts dust. Buy special bicycle oil at a bike shop. Sturmey-Archer oil is a brand that many cyclists use.

Oil all of the bike's exposed moving parts, including the freewheel, the pivot bolts that hold the front and rear derailleurs in place, and the brake-lever pivot bolts. Apply the oil sparingly. Plan on doing the job about once a month.

Many riders also oil their bike chains. But it's better to apply a dry lubricant (purchased at a bike shop) to the chain. It is longer lasting and it attracts less dust.

Don't plan on using any grease on your bike. Sure, the wheel bearings, the bottom bracket, headset, and rear fork all require grease, but this is a job that should be handled by a bike shop mechanic. Never, no matter what, use oil on these parts.

REMOVING AND REPLACING WHEELS—Wheels have to be removed to fix flats and for a variety of other reasons. When you need to remove one (and you don't have a bikestand), simply turn the bike upside down, letting it rest on the seat and handlebars.

With bike upside down, wheel slips easily out of drop slots.

Removing the front wheel is a cinch, particularly if the bike is equipped with quick-release hubs. You only have to flip the lever on each side of the hub, then pull the wheel free.

If you don't have quick-release levers, six-sided nuts will be used to hold the wheel to the front fork. Unwind both of these at the same time, turning each in a counterclockwise direction. There will be washers behind the nuts. Remember, when you're putting the wheel back on, the washers go between the bolts and the fork dropouts.

The rear wheel is a bit more difficult. You have to remove the chain from the freewheel sprocket, which means first riding the chain onto the smallest sprocket. Then flip the levers or undo the nuts. Pull

the wheel out. If you can do this with one hand, hold the derailleur back with the other hand so the freewheel clears easily; otherwise, gently wiggle it free.

When replacing the rear wheel, first work the axle into the drop-out slots. Slip the chain over the smallest sprocket on the freewheel. Set the levers or turn the nuts so light pressure is applied, then pull the wheel toward the rear of the bike until the ends of the axle come in contact with the back of the drop-out slots. Last, tighten the levers or nuts.

CLEANING AND LUBRICATING THE CHAIN—This is a chore that you should perform every few months, oftener if you ride long distances regularly, say, an average of 75 to 100 miles a week. A clean, well-lubricated chain assures easy pedaling.

To clean the chain, you have to take it off the bike, and to do this you have to open a link. The chains for derailleur bikes have no master links (as chains on nonderailleurs do). A special chain-link

Special tool is required to separate chain links.

54

remover is required to take the chain apart and put it back together. This tool can be purchased at a bike shop for less than $5.

Lay the chain across the link remover, centering its prong exactly on the rivet. Twist the handle, driving the rivet out. But do not push the rivet all the way through. While you want the two links to separate, you also want the rivet to remain in place. This makes it much easier to put the link back together.

Once the link is separated, slip the chain off the sprockets. Place it in a metal container, such as a coffee can. Pour in enough kerosene or paint thinner to cover the chain. Either of these will soften the dirt and grime that cover the chain, enabling you to remove it easily. (Don't use gasoline as a solvent; it's too dangerous.)

After the chain has soaked for ten or twenty minutes, take a toothbrush and scrub each link. Also use the toothbrush and solvent to clean the gunk off the teeth of the chainwheel and freewheel.

Once the chain is clean, dry it with a rag, then replace it on the sprockets. Adjust the chain so the separated links meet at the center of the length that stretches between the freewheel and chainwheel. This will give you room enough to operate the chain-link tool in rejoining the links. You simply fit the links together and place them in the tool in a reversed position.

The next step is to lubricate the chain. A good lubricant to use is Lubriplate, available at bike

Chain lubricant sprays on.

shops. It goes on easily and does not attract dust.

CHANGING A FLAT TIRE—Fixing a flat tire is easy to do. And it is a task that you should be able to accomplish anywhere, on the road as well as at home.

If the tube is merely punctured, that is, if it hasn't suffered a gaping wound, it can be patched. You need a patching kit plus a set of tire irons to do the work. Both can be purchased at a bike shop for just a few dollars.

Before you start looking for the puncture and making the repairs, check the valve of the afflicted tire. That may be the source of the trouble. Remove the cap and place a drop of spit at the end of the valve stem. If there's a leak in the valve, the spit will bubble. Simply tightening the valve (with the top of the valve cap) may solve the problem.

If it's not the valve, spin the wheel and look for the trouble spot. Remove the piece of glass or tack or whatever else caused the puncture, then

Use tire irons in removing tire and tube from rim.

Mark the punctured spot.

mark the spot with a piece of chalk (usually provided in the patch kit).

Remove the wheel, and deflate the tire. Then remove the locknut that holds the valve in place.

Work the tire back and forth by pressing and squeezing with your hands in an effort to get the bead free of the rim. If the tire loosens sufficiently, you may be able to remove it from the rim with your hands, lifting a small section over the rim first, and eventually working it completely off.

But the chances are you will have to use tire irons. Be careful not to pinch the tube when inserting the irons, or you could have additional punctures to repair.

Insert the first iron under the bead, or tire edge, and pry it over the rim. Leaving the iron in place,

move several inches to the right or left, and make a second pry. A third pry, several inches from the second, may also be necessary.

Once the bead is off the rim, remove the tube, first marking the punctured spot. If you don't know where the puncture is located, inflate the tube and rotate it past your ear, listening for the hiss of escaping air. Mark the puncture and deflate the tube.

Repair the tube with the patch kit. The directions will instruct you to clean the tube in the area of the puncture, roughen it with an abrasive (provided in the kit), apply cement, then press a patch onto the cemented area.

If you haven't yet determined what caused the puncture, try to find out before you replace the tire.

Apply the patch.

Run your fingers around the inside of the casing in search of an embedded piece of glass. Check the spoke ends to be sure none is protruding. If the puncture happens to be on the inside of the tube, it could be a spoke that caused it.

Before replacing the tube, inflate it most of the way to get the wrinkles and folds out of it. Push the valve stem through its hole in the rim, then loop the tube around the rim edge and stuff it under the tire. Replace the valve stem locknut, but don't tighten it all the way yet.

Push the beaded edge of the tire back onto the rim with your hands, being careful not to pinch the tube between the tire edge and the rim.

As you get near the end, it will get harder and harder to get the bead over the rim. The last couple

Use your hands to press the bead over the rim.

of inches will be especially tough, but don't resort to the use of a tire iron unless you absolutely have to; you risk puncturing the tube. Using your thumbs,

You may have to use tire irons to get the last few inches over the rim.

first from one side, then the other, keep squeezing until there's only an inch or so remaining. Then make one last, all-out effort and pop it on.

Tighten the valve locknut, pump the tire to full pressure, replace the wheel, and you're ready to go.

ADJUSTING THE BRAKES—There are two do-it-yourself brake adjustments you can make. You can tighten the brake cables as they stretch, and you can realign the brake shoes (the pads that come in contact with the rim) when they fail to hit the rim squarely.

Brake cables stretch with use and age. You can tell when they need tightening with this test: Squeeze the brake levers as hard as you can. If you then find that there's less than one inch of clearance between either lever and the handlebars, tightening is necessary.

To make a brake-cable adjustment, look for the adjusting sleeve, a pair of rings usually located at the wheel-end of the brake cable. Loosen the lock-ring or nut, and then turn the adjusting sleeve counterclockwise until the cable is tightened sufficiently. Then retighten the locknut.

If the adjusting sleeve turns all the way and the cable is still loose, there's another step involved. You must loosen the cable anchor bolt and pull more cable through. This requires a wrench (to undo the bolt) and a pair of pliers (to pull the cable).

You also can use the help of a friend. Have your friend hold the brake shoes tight to the rim as you

Loosening a brake-cable adjusting screw

pull the cable through. Then retighten the bolt and test the brakes. If you pulled too much cable through, the pads won't release from the rim. Turn the adjusting sleeve until the cable length is right.

Be sure to check both the front and rear cables. If both should need adjustment, tackle the front cable first. Operations at the front wheel are somewhat simpler than at the rear. By making the front-wheel adjustments first, you gain experience and confidence for the more difficult rear wheel.

Adjusting the brake shoes is a bit more complicated than adjusting the cable, yet it shouldn't cause you any real difficulty. There are two brake shoes at the front wheel, and two at the rear. Each takes the form of a small metal rectangle that holds a rubber pad. The holder is attached to the brake arm by means of a bolt-and-nut assembly.

When you squeeze the brake levers, each pair of shoes should contact the rim squarely. No part of any pad should touch a tire; no part should hang below the rim.

To adjust the pads, loosen the nut just a little bit, and tap the shoe until it slides into the correct position. Then retighten the nut. Be careful not to use too much force when you retighten, because the bolt is easily stripped.

When the shoes get worn down, replace the whole unit, both the holders and the shoes. There are many different sizes available, so take one of the old units with you to be sure you get the right size.

Sometimes problems with braking are caused, not by worn or misaligned brake shoes, but by a wheel that is out of line. Turn the bike upside down and spin the wheel. Check to see that the rim on both sides stays the same distance from the pads throughout each revolution. If the distances are unequal at points, the wheel may be bent and have to be trued. This is a job that should be performed by a mechanic. Or maybe you should buy a new wheel.

ADJUSTING THE DERAILLEURS—Take a close look at your bike's front derailleur. There is a metal cage through which the chain passes as it feeds onto the sprocket. The cage moves from one side to the other, and in so moving it shifts the chain from one sprocket to the other.

Derailleurs are fitted with two adjustment screws that control the movement of the cages. For example, if the chain, when feeding onto the inside chainwheel, moves so far to the left it slips off, you tighten the low-gear screw (the screw on the left). If the chain feeds so far to the right that it slips off the large chainwheel, tighten the high-gear screw (the one on the right).

The rear derailleur has a pair of similar adjustment screws.

Adjusting the rear derailleur

Of course, there are many other repairs and adjustments you can make yourself. Most of these, however, require a detailed knowledge of the bicycle and its parts, plus more than an average amount of mechanical skill.

If you plan to do any major work, be sure to consult a repair manual first. Two of the best and most readily available are:

• *Richard's Bicycle Book*, by Richard Ballantine. Ballentine Books, New York, 1982.

• *DeLong's Guide to Bicycles and Bicycling*, by Fred DeLong. Chilton Book Co., Radnor, PA, 1978.

The alternative to doing it yourself, of course, is to take your bike to the local bike repair shop. Most shops are reputable, but some are not. If you don't have a personal knowledge of a shop, ask another bike owner to recommend one to you.

Once the work has been completed, check it right away. If it isn't right, complain. Don't accept the bike until the work meets your satisfaction.

FOR MORE INFORMATION

Whether you happen to be interested in 3-speed bikes or 10-speeders, in unicycles or tandems, in racing, touring, or recreational riding, there is a cycling organization ready to provide you with information about your speciality. Here's a rundown:

AMERICAN BICYCLE ASSOCIATION
P.O. Box 718
Chandler, AZ 85224

An organization that sanctions BMX races and provides background information on the sport.

AMERICAN YOUTH HOSTELS
National Office
1332 I Street N.W., Suite 800
Washington, DC 20005

With chapters in most cities of the United States, the AYH is a nonprofit organization that offers low-cost domestic and international tours.

BICYCLE MANUFACTURERS ASSOCIATION OF AMERICA
1055 Thomas Jefferson Street N.W.
Washington, DC 20007

A trade association of about 20 companies that manufacture bicycles and bicycle parts, the BMAA seeks to promote increased bicycle use; provides many different free booklets on various aspects of riding and racing. Write for a free list of publications and educational materials.

BIKECENTENNIAL
P.O. Box 8308
Missoula, MT 59807

An organization that runs bike tours and maps long-distance bike routes; publishes a magazine devoted to touring and sells maps and other touring information.

CANADIAN CYCLING ASSOCIATION
333 River Road
Vanier City, K1L 8B9 Canada

Founded in 1882, this organization is extremely active in both competitive and recreational cycling. It provides information on touring in Canada, sponsors and promotes junior racing, and provides the Canadian cycling teams for the Pan-American Games and Olympic Games. The organization publishes many different booklets about cycling; write for a free publication list.

CANADIAN HOSTELING ASSOCIATION
18 The Byward Market
Ottawa K1N 7A1 Canada

The Canadian counterpart of American Youth Hostels.

LEAGUE OF AMERICAN WHEELMEN
P.O. Box 988
Baltimore, MD 21203

This century-old organization of more than 20,000 bicycle enthusiasts of all ages conducts a variety of programs, including touring events, encourages the use of bicycles for transportation, represents the interests of cyclists before local, state, and federal governments, and also publishes a monthly magazine, *The American Wheelman*.

NATIONAL BICYCLE LEAGUE
84 Park Avenue
Flemington, NJ 08822

An organization that sanctions BMX races and provides background information about the sport.

PROFESSIONAL RACING ORGANIZATION
1524 Linden Street
Allentown, PA 18102

The governing body of professional bicycle racing in the United States.

TANDEM CLUB OF AMERICA
Route 1, Box 276
Esperance, NY 12066

For owners of bicycles built for two or more persons, this organization sponsors regional rallies and publishes a newsletter.

ULTRA-MARATHON CYCLING ASSOCIATION
Suite 152
358 Main Street
Orange, CA 92668

This organization runs long-distance cycling events, including the Race Across America, and publishes the *Ultra-Marathon Cycling Manual.*

UNICYCLING SOCIETY OF AMERICA
P.O. Box 40534
Redford, MI 48240

For owners of one-wheeled, pedal-driven machines, the USA promotes unicycling and publishes a quarterly newsletter.

UNITED STATES CYCLING FEDERATION
1750 East Boulder Street
Colorado Springs, CO 80909

The governing body of amateur racing in the U.S. and the organization that sponsors national championship competition, the USCF encourages cycling as a recreational activity and promotes the safety education of all cyclists. It has a membership of more than 15,000.

GLOSSARY

ABA—The American Bicycle Association, one of the organizations that governs BMX racing.

BARS—Short for handlebars.

BEAD—The wire, within the outside edge of the tire.

BERM—A high-banked turn.

BMX—Abbreviation for bicycle motocross.

BOTTOM BRACKET—The short tube at the bottom of the bicycle frame into which the crank axle and crank bearings fit.

BRAKE LEVER—The part of the brake system mounted on the handlebars that activates the caliper brakes.

BRAKE SHOES—The pads that provide the friction that brakes the wheels.

CALIPER BRAKES—Hand brakes; they are operated by handelbar-mounted levers.

CHAIN—The unit that transmits power from the chainwheel (or front sprocket) to the rear wheel.

CHAIN STAYS—The section of the bicycle frame from the bottom bracket to the rear-wheel dropouts.

CHAINWHEEL—The large wheel with gear teeth on the right crank that delivers power from the pedal and crank, through the chain, to the rear wheel. Also called the front sprocket.

CLINCHER—A type of tire common to lightweight bikes which has a removable inner tube.

COASTER BRAKE—A bicycle brake activated by back pressure on the pedals.

CONES—The bearings on opposite sides of the axle that hold the wheel in place.

CRANK—The metal rotating arm to which the pedal attaches.

CRUISER—A 1-speed bike.

DERAILLEUR—From the French word meaning "derail," the type of gear system common to 10-speed bikes in which the drive chain switches from one sprocket to another when you shift.

DOWN TUBE—The part of the bicycle frame that extends from the head tube to the bottom bracket.

DROPOUT—A slot at the bottom of a fork and stay into which an axle fits.

FREESTYLE—Trick riding.

FREEWHEEL—The rear sprocket; also called the cog.

FRONT FORK—The steering assembly that holds the front wheel.

FRONT SPROCKET—*See* Chainwheel

GEAR RATIO—A number that tells you how many times the rear wheel will revolve for every revolution of the pedals. The gear ratio is found by dividing the number of teeth in the chainwheel by the number of teeth in the rear sprocket.

GENDER BAR—The top tube, the horizontal tube that extends from the steering head to the seat tube. (It is called the gender bar because it is what distinguishes a boy's bike from a girl's.)

GOOSENECK—*See* Handlebar stem

GUSSET—A metal brace added at a joint as reinforcement.

HANDLEBAR STEM—The clamp that holds the handlebars; the bottom part of the stem fits into the head tube. Also called the gooseneck or stem.

HEAD—*See* Head tube

HEADSET—The bearing assembly within the steering head.

HEAD TUBE—The large-diameter metal tube that holds the front fork and bearings. Also called the steering head.

HUB—The units within the front and rear wheels which house the bearings and axles and hold the spoke ends.

MIXTE FRAME—A bike frame without any top tube, but which instead features a pair of metal struts that extend from the headset to the rear hub.

MOTOCROSS—A motorcycle race over rugged terrain. The term comes from "motorcycle" and "cross-country."

PANNIERS—Bicycle saddlebags, usually slung over the bike's rear rack.

PURSUIT—Cycling competition in which contestants dual on a rider vs. rider or team vs. team basis.

RIM—The outer circle of the bicycle wheel.

SADDLE—The bicycle seat.

SANCTION—The authorization for holding a race meet according to established rules and regulations.

SANCTIONED RACE—Race conducted under an association's rules and regulations.

SEAT POST—The metal rod that holds the seat. The bottom end of the seat post fits into the seat tube.

SEAT STAYS—The parts of the bicycle frame that extend from beneath the seat to the rear-wheel axle and drop-outs.

SEAT TUBE—The metal tube into which the seat post fits. It extends from beneath the seat to the bottom bracket.

SEW-UP—A type of tire common to racing bikes in which the inner tube is sewn in and cannot be removed.

SPROCKET—A toothed, chain-driven wheel.

STEERING HEAD—*See* Head tube

STEM—*See* Handlebar stem

TANDEM—A bicycle built for more than one person.

TIME TRIAL—Cycling competition in which contestants race against the clock.

TOP TUBE—The horizontal metal tube that extends from the steering head to the seat tube.

TOURING—Taking a long bicycle trip.

UNICYCLE—A one-wheeled bike.

VELODROME—A steeply banked track for bike racing.

WHEELIE—A trick in which you ride with the front wheel off the ground.